Bea Lauren Reid

Shades of Blue & Yellow

A Poetry Collection

Contents

Prologue:

. How To Be A Poet

Summer:

. Orange Juice Days

. Rain

. A Summer's Day: 2008

. This Place

. Things That I Found

. Time Travel In Hockley Woods

. Wild Ones

. Coming Home

. How Do You Tell Her?

. Do You Still Wear Pink Trainers?

Autumn:

. Smokestacks

. Colour Me Whole

. How To Live

. Sunset Upon Summer

. Tapestry

. One Day I Woke Up

. Shades Of Blue & Yellow

. Forests

. How To Eat A Poem

. Morning Song

Winter:

. One-Hundred Names

. Before The Coffee Gets Cold

. Harvest Of The Broken

. One, Two, Three

. Seasons

. I Walked

. I Am Not A Dandelion

. Tell Me Where The Lonely Ends

. Breath Of April

. The Table

Spring:

. Honey and Sugar

. How?

. I Like You, Like

. Novels

. I Found True Love In My Latte

. Hair

. Five Times That I Loved You

. Things I Have Lost

. Teeth

. Love Was Half A Kit-Kat

Epilogue:

. Places

Acknowledgments:

. Thank You

. About The Author

Prologue

How To Be A Poet

1. Inhale
2. Wait until the world falls into your palms
3. Exhale

Summer

Orange Juice Days

Here's to the orange juice days.

The eternal summer,
star struck wonder,
days of orange juice rain.

The days when we awoke at dawn
with adventure in our bones,
and powered our souls with stories
that we dug up in our gardens
and pulled down from blushing skies.

Here's to the orange juice days.

The days of popping flower bulbs
and twisting cherry stems
with ruby stained tongues,
the days of toothpaste grins,
our feet bare and our hair wild

Here's to the orange juice days.

The friendships forged on butter candies,
love declared in dandelion bouquets.
The days of every day is yours,
of happily ever afters
and *we'll play again tomorrow*'s

Yes, here's to the orange juice days.

Those days from years gone by.
Now flickers of a life once lived,
a world once known.

Remembered fondly over
morning coffee;

the morning coffee days
where I live now.

Rain

When I was six,
an old lady told me
that each time it rained,
the sky poured out life
to the flowers down below.
Hand in hand with the sun,
to raise them up
into something strong and beautiful.

And so, sometimes
When the skies tore themselves open
I would go, eager.
And stand bare-foot on the patio,
palms upturned, eyes closed
thinking to myself,

Now, I'm certain
I will grow in that way too.

A Summer's Day: 2008

It was the three of us,
messy plaits and stripy shorts and
bare legs stretched across hot pavement.
Lemon ice-creams at our lips and
fistfuls of daisies scattered at our feet.

We had the world plus many more
at our muddied fingertips and
our dreams were merely solid plans
we were sure that we would keep.

And although, no.
I did not become the queen or
move to disney world,
and you do not train dolphins
or live in a submarine.

But a part of me, today
even still,
harbours dreams unshaken
from our now
faded
childhood days.

This Place

Welcome back to this old world,
the place that we called home.
These streets are paved with memories
of the girl I used to know.

The leaves and grass they whisper
of the way things used to be,
of summers spent soaked in the sun,
legs dangling out of trees.

The clouds they tell a story,
of the people come and gone.
The seaside sounds a symphony
of this place where we come from.

The houses that reside here,
harbour lives we used to live.
Of tears and hope and laughter
that we loved and held and miss.

So if you listen carefully,
then this town will let you know.
of lemon scented childhood days
when we called this place home.

Things That I Found

Things that I found whilst clearing out my childhood bedroom//

The stories I wrote when I was six. All scribbled crayon and misspelled words
/ My first pair of shoes / The blush pink dress I wore to prom four years ago /
The stuffed rabbit (I called her Spotty) I cherished until I was eleven /
Some seashells from Cornwall / My Year 9 science book

The diary I kept when I was fifteen, filled with secrets and heartbreaks and
since forgotten dreams / An empty box of chocolates / The coffee stained patch
of carpet I spent six years trying to hide / The first lipstick I ever bought
(and hated the colour of) / Piles of memories in the form of letters and post it notes /

The realisation I will never be a child again / The socks he left at my house
/ My old school tie / The reality of now

Having to say goodbye / The responsibility of
simply. letting. go.

And finding the courage to tomorrow, say

hello

once again.

Time Travel In Hockley Woods

When I go down to the woods,
I am ten years old.

I sing softly to the trees and
harmonise with the breath
of the earth
twisting through its leaves

Lips and fingertips stained purple
from the wild blackberries
twixt the brambles and
eyes and heart set skyward
through its emerald canopies.

And when I stop by the river,
I am not of this earth.

I am at one with the dirt,
and the birds,
and the thicket.

And I am more than myself,
And less than myself,
All at once.

So when I go down to the woods,
for just one small moment,
I am, quite simply
free.

Wild Ones

We were flurries of
pink stripes and
sticky ice-cream chins.

We were untethered from
the world and at one
with our dreams.

We were the unbroken.

The sea-soaked,
sun-sodden,
summers of some
seasons ago.

And someday?
We may be those
wild ones
once again.

Coming Home

When Saturday mornings taste like sugared cornflakes
and not yesterday's wine,
it's like coming home.

When Mum calls you down for dinner,
and not because it's been too long,
it's like coming home.

When radiators press against cold feet,
and fingers are sticky with pancake syrup,
and your duvet is an island,
it's like coming home.

And when Grandad pops round to fix the cupboard,
and Grandma has made a Victoria Sponge,
it's like coming home.

And when at night,
you lay awake and spot the smudged mascara in the carpet
and remember being seventeen,
and when the faces of your parents have changed,
but the mugs and the plates
are still the same,

it's always like coming home.

How Do You Tell Her?

How do you face a child, aged ten,
and tell her,
life won't always work out the way you want it to?

How do you take her dreams,
and tell her she should aim for something else?

How do you take the balloon from her hands
and say,
there are more important things now?

But most of all,
how can you face yourself,
right now,
and not see a child, aged ten,
staring back?

Do You Still Wear Pink Trainers?

Hello there, me at twenty-one!
It's you at eleven here!
I am so excited to ask you
about what you are like now.

Is your bedroom still purple?
I hope so.
We like purple.
The same colour
as our favourite sweets!

Do you have any pets?
We have some goldfish right now.
Do you have a dog?
PLEASE tell me we have a dog!

Are you in love yet?
I hope so!
It must be just like
in Cinderella, surely?

How are your friends?
I'm sure we are all still besties!
Did you ever get that friendship bracelet back?

WAIT!
I almost forgot!
What about your story?
The one about the dragons?
Did you send it to the place
Where they make them into books?

What else....What else.....

Oh, right!

Did we save up our pocket money
to buy that ukulele?
The girl in the year above has one,
And I think we'd like one too.

Do you still wear pink trainers?
We swore we'd never wear anything
but *pink* trainers.
Please tell me
you kept all the promises we made
to ourselves?

Autumn

Smokestacks

Hazy winter hue hangs half-hidden
in cold-cracked cobalt dusk

I am but one,
amongst the blurry figures
moving quickly, heads bowed down,
eyes averted from the stare
of this pin-curled cloud descending
like smokestacks to the sky

with fingers pressed into palms,
I wonder why the bitter breath of January
craves my skin like moths to the moon.

And with the song of seasons new
brewing gently in my chest,

I tilt my chin towards my heart
and head towards
the ever breaking light.

Colour Me Whole

When I'm at peace and my mind is still
my heart is powdered blue and teal,
When joy is deep within my bones,
 instead it's yellow, gold and chrome.

When passion floods my heart and veins,
my soul is amber scarlet flames
When inspiration floods my all
viridian will deluge my whole

When i am lost and falling down
my mind is charcoal umber brown.
When fear draws in and pulls me back,
my skies turn smoky bister black.

When laughter spills out to my toes,
my life's a saffron summer rose.
When I'm between the earth and sky
I just see olive, sage and pine.

And when i rest in heavenly heights,
I am made technicolour bright.
For when into these arms I fall,
a world of colour fills my all.

How To Live

1. Go out, alone, early in the morning to the quietest part of the forest, or the very edge of the sea

2. Shout out to the sky 'what is it I am made to do?'

3. Close your eyes and listen. Very, very carefully.

4. Wait until you hear something

5. Go and do likewise.

Sunset Upon Summer

Summertide grapples at the sun-split clouds,
and we watch with open mouths and peach-juice chins
as she retreats into her long-due slumber.

And we wait.
Visions of drowsy trees and their terracotta veils,
our eager eyes set softly above
and our hearts awaiting silver frosted dawns.

We wait.
Until the skies exhale,
and the harvest comes tumbling in.

Wait.
Patient til our lungs are filled
at last
with a sweet September song.

Tapestry

How often do we get the chance
to really,
really,
feel?

Lips curled into morning coffee,
fingers wrapped round mugs,
the sun upon our waking faces?
the air inside our lungs?

Do we swallow down worlds held in our hands,
and savour every single word?
Do we drink in melodies
and get drunk on sweet normalities?

Do we notice the earth beneath our feet,
And see the world above our heads?
Listen to the way the trees
sing of centuries gone by,
and trace with our fingers the tapestry
of nature's ceaseless symphony.

Or do we waste the passing hours,
whilst we weather
waging wars?

Waiting for the magic
that already
so sweetly surrounds us.

One Day I Woke Up

One day I woke up and I had become the Moon.

I skimmed the edge of the stars,
and had a cup of tea with Saturn.

I watched the passing comets,
and waded through the oceans
of the earth.

And as nightfall passed my bedroom window,
I tumbled forwards over the carpet,
and back beneath the duvet.

And I hoped that tomorrow,
perhaps,
I might finally wake as the Sun.

Shades of Blue & Yellow

Paint a picture of a person

The teacher told us.

And try to tell their story, through what you paint.

And so I painted,
in shades of blue and yellow.
Sapphire and mustard.
Indigo and lemon.

Until I stopped.
Stood back.
And somewhere,
somehow,
I recognised myself.

Forests

If you go deep into the forest
and wait softly by the river,
you might hear the stories that
they whisper.
Of boatmen and pond skaters,
of submerged toes and
bare-armed breaststrokes.
They might tell you of the thirsty
who passed by,
and of the gliding ducks and
kingfishers,
swept up in ribbons of green.
Or they might tell you of their heart,
twixt the lungs of the hills,
and how they carved veins
between the evergreens
and burst breath into the sea.
And maybe they will wait
and hope you notice too,
that they raised the trees and oceans
and gave time
just to tell you so.

How To Eat A Poem

I lick poetry from my lips,
like salty kisses.

Savour a metaphor on my tongue
and swallow the universe whole and
drink down the cherry wine fantasy
of a far off tomorrow.

Until i am left,
full and thankful

of bittersweet,
content.

Morning Song

Morning light seeps softly in
and dances there
upon my skin
And flowing through
the open doors,
the first light sky-borne
overture
of birds that burst forth
from the trees,
and pull the light across
the seas.

And as we stir from
tangled beds,
we lift our rested
weary heads.
And watch the world
rise in its way,
that welcomes in
the breaking day.

Winter

One Hundred Names

I have been given one-hundred names in my life.

The one they gave me at birth.
Strong, simple,
the one that most people know.

But later,
there were others too.

Little girl.
Girl with the plaits.
The quiet girl.
The girl whose Dad died.
The girl who cries a lot.

Then a few years later.

I can't believe she has a crush on him.
(Did you see her face when he rejected her?!)
The nice girl.
(She's kind of quiet though)
A quiet and conscientious student.
A little away with the fairies.

And later still.

Let the nice lady past, darling!

Bitch.
Boring.
Ugly.

(I guess she could pass for a seven.)
Excuse me madam, you can't stand there!

Cute.
Kind.
Pretty.

Oh yeah, I remember her. She sat behind me in science I think.

Friend.
Daughter.
Leader.

And I wonder.
How many names the world has left to give me.

Before The Coffee Gets Cold

And in the smallish hours
at the sweet ascent of dawn,
just before the coffee gets cold,
I stop and smile at the morning sky.

It is there that I find comfort
in the soft blur
of half-light
half-awake
half-true
wholly mine

moments of reverie.

Harvest Of The Broken

This season is not one for celebration.
There is no feast,
no golden reward,
no blooming fruits,
no smiling lips,
no frostbitten toes.

There is no harvest in the desert.
Only ravenous lips,
hungry for the memory
of something once
wonderfully sweet.

One, Two, Three

One, Two, Three.
Name five things you can see.

The swaying dandelion clocks, shedding their manes.
The lady stood putting on lipstick (or maybe smoking a cigarette)
My trembling hands clutching crumpled tissues
Grass, slightly yellowed
Feet, tapping frantically the floor

Three, Two, One
Four things you can touch

My knees
My elbows
My face
My lips

Four, Five, Six
Three things you can hear

My heartbeat in my ears,
The seagulls (or maybe i'm screaming?)
The shouting in my head

Six, Five, Four
Two things you can smell.

The smoke from the lady's cigarette
The dregs of my coffee shop latte

Seven, Eight Nine,
One thing you can taste.

The bittersweetness of the fact
I've found myself here again
for the third time this week.

Ten.
Do it all again

Seasons

When the season feels uncertain
and your roots are tied and bound,
consider how the wildflowers
spring up freely from the ground.

And even in the waiting,
when you're scared to take up room,
stay rooted and be patient dear,
you will grow and flower soon.

I Walked

I've walked ten miles with sadness,
I've walked ten miles with pain,
I've walked ten miles with fear and doubt
and I will walk those paths again.

But I also walk with boldness,
and I also walk with love.
Each day I walk with hope and joy
and faith within my blood.

I've hiked the paths of happiness,
and seen each rainstorm through,
And, my dear, I one day hope
I'll walk those paths with you.

I Am Not A Dandelion

I am not a dandelion,
I am a mighty tree.
And I am firmly rooted deep
In who I'm meant to be.

Tell Me Where The Lonely Ends

Tell me when the lonely ends,
in the arms of a lover?
In the kindness of a friend?
Or low between a star soaked sky,
tell me when the lonely ends.

Tell me where the lonely rests,
deep in my bones?
Lodged in my chest?
Brewing in a wandering soul,
tell me where the lonely rests.

Tell me what the lonely sing
Of empty words?
Or un-spread wings?
Waiting, longing, to take flight,
Tell me what the lonely sing.

Tell me how the lonely leaves.
When breathless prayers
become the truth I breathe.
When at long last the sun will rise,
Tell me how the lonely leaves.

So, tell me where the happy lies,
with lazy mornings?
In springtime skies?
Tell me, when is it all worthwhile?
Tell me (please)
Where the happy lies?

Breath of April

Rake in the winter leaves
from my lungs
and watch as life
springs forth
again.

The Table*

A girl full of the curiosity for life comes home,
puts her bag on the table,
puts down her books, her keys,
her half-drank latte in a paper cup.
On the table she puts her coat,
on-top of that, her scarf, her hat, her gloves.
She takes the sunshine from her chest,
and puts that down too.
The lady who smiled at her on the train,
the man singing in the town centre,
the smile on her face.
Onto the table the girl puts
the sixteen times she sighed,
the eight times she lied,
his name, his words, his smile.
She puts down the clouds,
the puddles,
the sky,
a tremble here and there,
but she holds it still,
and piles on more and more.

* This poem is from an exercise from the book *How To Grow Your Own Poem* by Kate Clanchy
  and is a rewrite of a poem by Edip Cansever.

Spring

Sugar & Honey

Your voice was melted butter and
dark caramel.
Your sticky honey words like
donut sugar on my lips,
impossible to resist the craving
to lick them up
and savour their sticky sweetness,
then be left longing for more.

How?

How is it we came so close?
So close to all that we had hoped.
So close to all that we had dreamed.
So close to what we both so clearly knew.
But your words could never
come quite close enough.

I Like You Like

I like you,

like the smell of after rain, the sun between the clouds and the symphony of seven am. like cherry stones and grass stained knees, like bookshops and canal boats and strawberry iced tea.

I like you like the freckle on my cheek, the way that the ocean never stills. like pockets and raincoats and mountains. like fingers dipped in sugar and sand stuck to our feet.

I like you like home. soft and gentle, peach and lilac hue. like fresh sheets and shaved legs and cinnamon pasties from paper bags.

I like you,

like each moment was embroidered with silver thread, and a momentary flicker of the promise of a golden tomorrow.

Novels

Let us live on this page here / the one with sun upon our skin / the sand between our toes / salted air in sprightly lungs / stomachs lined with ketchup laden chips / the sweeping ceaseless sky / the smell of candy floss and / lemon coloured joy.

Let us not turn the page / the breaking of the spine / the falling of night / the closing of the door / the empty mugs on tabletops / the waiting for the sun to rise / the longing for the salted air and / yearning for a youthful sky / once more

Or maybe / maybe? / look ahead / and tell me / how the story ends.

I Found True Love In My Latte

Each day,
I fall in love with
all that I hoped love
would be.

I find it there,
in coffee rings on countertops
and tea-stained lips
that speak of something
shaped like hope.

It comes, unexpected
like the rain upon my skin,
and whispers of the sun
whose glory days
for which we wait.

And I can hear it.
Wrapped in minor chords
and melancholy melodies,
so softly sung to say goodbye
to a slow descending day.

Until at last
we meet again,
for the very
first
time.

Hair

Your hair has grown since we last met.

And perhaps gone more curly,
or maybe turned more brown.

And I cannot tell if it is
just the time that's passed
since those glory days
that are a dagger in my chest

Or if it is the way I am reminded
once again
how I still long for something
far more than what
I already
had.

Five Times That I Loved You

Five: We are sixteen, smitten and slightly drunk, red wine stained lips and the
boreal sea lapping at our feet. You see me shiver, and offer me your coat, salt sprayed
hair caught in your eyes. I refuse but smile, feeling warmer just at your side.

Four: A cold and rainy saturday; you remember exactly how I like my tea. hot and
strong, a dash of milk. you let me cry and draw the rising panic from my chest,
your voice like honey to my soul.

Three: We sit, sprawled on the grass. drinking in the last of summer's sun and laughing until
the evening brims the hills. we recall the years gone by in the bittersweet glow of nostalgia and
your fingers gently skimming mine.

Two: You read to me your words from scribbled notebook pages. you redden,
and stumble over metaphors and imagery, the outpour of your heart
held in your twitching hands. you ask to hear my own, but I h
ad left my words at home.

One: The day it fell apart. I see the breaking in your eyes, a silent cry for all it
could have been, and all it nearly was. you hold me close and kiss my head and
whisper your goodbye. we part, but hope one day perhaps, our worlds will recollide.

Things I Have Lost

Things I have lost

The penny change from those custard tarts/ That photograph of us on the beach/
The letter you wrote that summer/ My favourite socks (the yellow ones with stripes)

My ability to listen to that song without thinking of you/ A piece of my heart
when you went away/ My house keys (on more than one occasion), The chords
 to that song I wrote

The chance to rewrite an ending/ The shells from Cornwall/ My words when
everything changed/ My sunglasses (I'm sure they're still in your car)

For a little while - my hope (of ever seeing you again)/ That night at that
party with the Pimm's cocktails/The name of that novel

You/ Us/ All that could have (should have?) been.

Teeth

You are stuck between my teeth,
wrapped around my tongue,
pressed between my lips.

And all I can taste
is the bittersweet nostalgia
of a life I never lived.

Love Was Half A Kit Kat

When I was seven,
love was a bundled bouquet of wild daisies
and half a kit-kat.
At fifteen,
tipsy kisses at parties
and a smile across the science classroom.

Today?

Maybe the way you made me realise
I'd never really known love
before today.

Epilogue

Places

But, oh, my dear!
The places you will go,
when you believe
that your feet
will take you there.

Acknowledgments

Thank You!

Thank You for buying and reading *Shades of Blue & Yellow!* I am so thankful that you're interested in the words I have written, and I hope it impacts you in some way too. Before I tell you a little more about myself, I want to give a few thank you's!

First of all, thank you to all of my friends and family who have been my fierce supporters for years, and have read and followed my writing journey all my life! I would never be still writing today without your encouragement. I also want to thank some of my school teachers from over the years! I've been lucky enough to have been cheered on by so many of them! As well as that, a big thank you to all of the poets and authors who I read and look up to, and who inspire me in my own work. There are far too many to name, but I'm thankful nonetheless!

And of course, I couldn't go without thanking the poetry community on Instagram, who have made this big jump to publish a book possible. You guys have inspired me with your own amazing poetry, and been such an encouragement to me as I started sharing my work online last year! Thank You to (as I write this) all 1422 of you!

I hope you've enjoyed this book, and you will treasure it. So, as I always say. Everyone has a story to tell, so go pick up your pens, and write.

About The Author

Bethany (Bea) Lauren Reid is a twenty-one year old writer from Southend-On-Sea in Essex, England. She has been writing since she was six years old, and has dreamed of becoming a published author since then. She is also currently studying for a degree in Theology, and has worked in Youth and Children's Ministry for more than six years. In her spare time, she loves to read, make music, and crochet.

Her work has also previously been printed in *#ESCAPRIL2019 Anthology Collection* in May 2019, and was shortlisted for the 2016 Felix Dennis Creative Writing Competition. She also posts some of her work on her Instagram (@bea.lauren.poetry).

She hopes to release more books in the future, including a YA novel and a Children's book.

Shades of Blue & Yellow is her first poetry collection.

"Tell me. What is it you plan to do with your one wild and precious life?"

— Mary Oliver

Printed in Great Britain
by Amazon

48745536R00036